SPACE MYSTERIES

HOW LONG WILL THE SUN LAST?

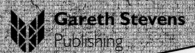 Gareth Stevens Publishing

BY MICHAEL SABATINO

Please visit our website, www.garethstevens.com. For a free color catalog of all our high-quality books, call toll free 1-800-542-2595 or fax 1-877-542-2596.

Library of Congress Cataloging-in-Publication Data

Sabatino, Michael.
How long will the sun last / by Michael Sabatino.
 p. cm. — (Space mysteries)
Includes index.
ISBN 978-1-4339-9224-7 (pbk)
ISBN 978-1-4339-9225-4 (6-Pack)
ISBN 978-1-4339-9223-0 (library binding)
1. Sun — Juvenile literature. 2. Astronomy — Juvenile literature. I. Title.
QB521.5 S23 2014
523.7—dc23

First Edition

Published in 2014 by
Gareth Stevens Publishing
111 East 14th Street, Suite 349
New York, NY 10003

Copyright © 2014 Gareth Stevens Publishing

Designer: Katelyn E. Reynolds
Editor: Therese Shea

Photo credits: Cover, p. 1 NASA/Tom Bridgman; cover, pp. 1, 3–32 (background texture) David M. Schrader/Shutterstock.com; pp. 3–32 (fun fact graphic) © iStockphoto.com/spxChrome; p. 5 Kirill Putchenko/E+/Getty Images; p. 7 NASA/Adler/U. Chicago/Wesleyan/JPL-Caltech; p. 9 NASA, ESA, S. Gallagher (University of Western Ontario), and J. English (University of Manitoba); p. 11 combination of far-infrared image ESA/Herschel/PACS/SPIRE/Hill, Motte, HOBYS Key Programme Consortium and X-ray image ESA/XMM-Newton/EPIC/XMM-Newton-SOC/Boulanger; p. 13 Mysid/Wikipedia.com; p. 15 NASA, ESA, and R. Humphreys (University of Minnesota); p. 17 Mehau Kulyk/Science Photo Library/Getty Images; p. 19 NASA/SDO (AIA)/Wikipedia.com; p. 21 NASA/ESA/G. Bacon; p. 23 Detlev van Ravenswaay/Picture Press/Getty Images; p. 25 ESA/NASA; p. 27. NASA/JPL-Caltech; p. 29 Matej Pavlansky/Shutterstock.com.

Printed in the United States of America

CPSIA compliance information: Batch #CS13GS: For further information contact Gareth Stevens, New York, New York at 1-800-542-2595.

CONTENTS

Words in the glossary appear in **bold** type the first time they are used in the text.

THE GIVING SUN

Can you imagine our world without the sun? It's hard to believe, but there once was a time when the sun didn't exist. So where did the sun come from? And if the sun had a beginning, when will it end?

From plants on Earth's surface to solar-powered **satellites** above us, much of our world depends on the sun. Without it, life as we know it wouldn't exist. But just how long can we expect the sun to last?

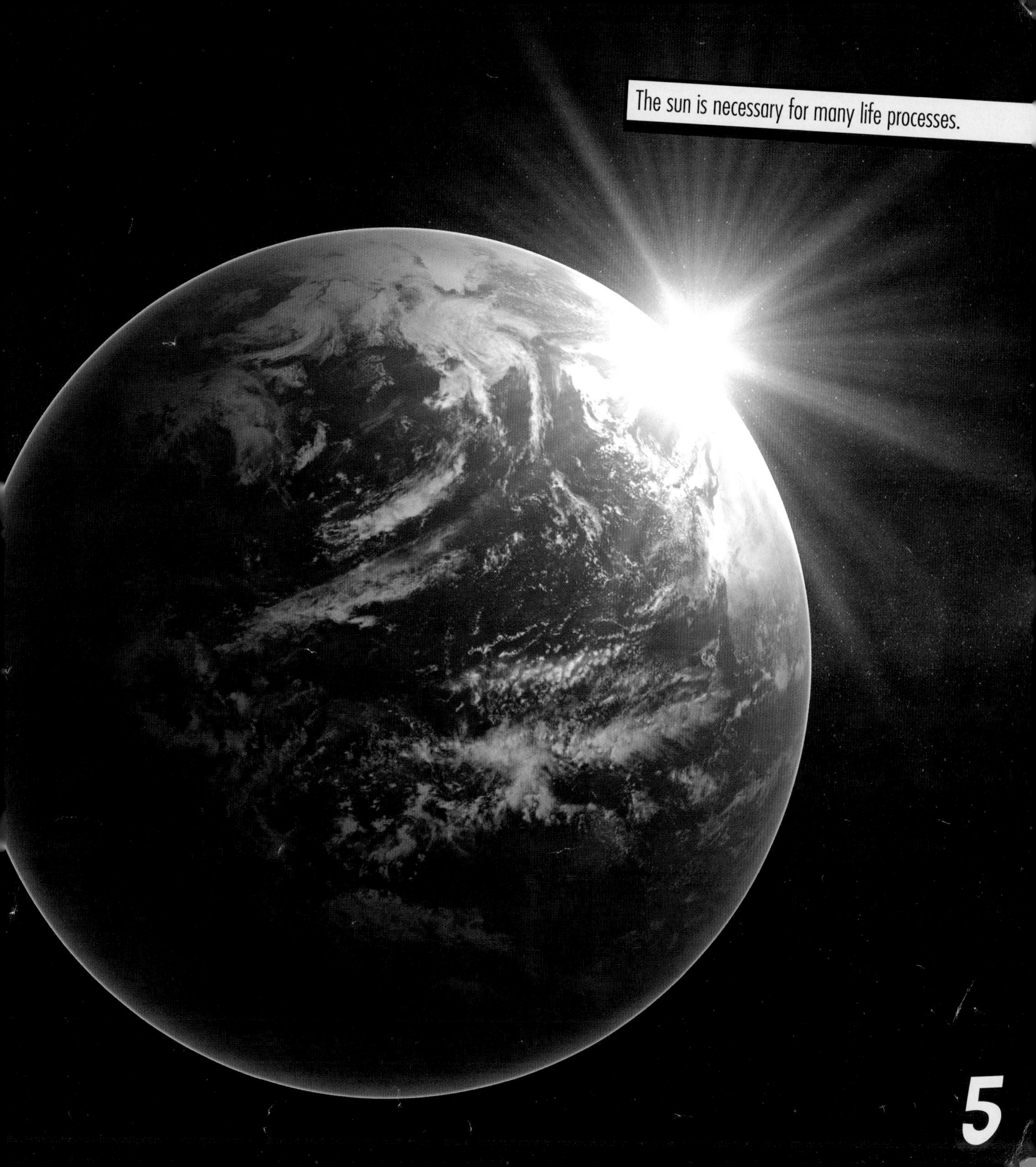

The sun is necessary for many life processes.

ONE OF MANY

On a clear night, nearly every star you can see with your naked eyes is located in our **galaxy**, called the Milky Way. The sun is just one of about 300 billion stars grouped together in the Milky Way galaxy. Galaxies can contain 10 million to 100 trillion stars.

We once thought our galaxy was all there was in the universe. Thanks to powerful telescopes that can see outside of our galaxy, it's thought there are at least 100 billion other galaxies out there!

OUT OF THIS WORLD!

Sunlight takes about 8 minutes to travel to Earth. If the sun just disappeared, we would still see it for 8 minutes!

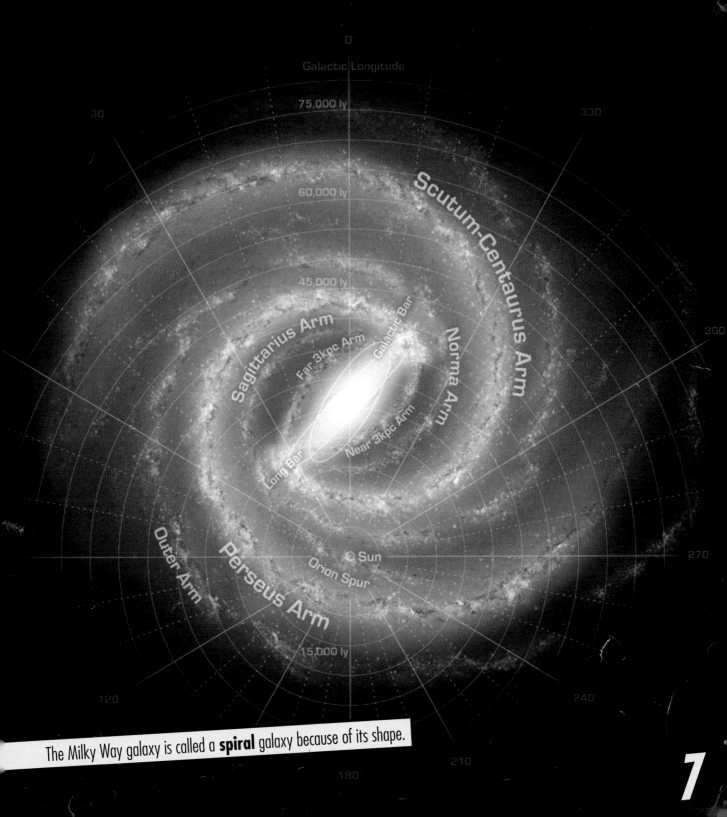

The Milky Way galaxy is called a **spiral** galaxy because of its shape.

A LONG TIME AGO

Stars are sort of like people. They're born, they live a number of years, and they die. Some are young, some are old, and they're many different sizes. Like people, each star has a **unique** form and a unique life.

Our sun got its start 4.6 billion years ago, but other stars are much older than that. The first stars were born more than 13 billion years ago. The universe itself was still young then.

OUT OF THIS WORLD!

Sunlight created deep in the center, or core, of the sun may take longer than 10,000 years to make its way to the surface.

This photo from the Hubble Space Telescope shows several ancient galaxies coming together. Some of the stars pictured are 10 billion years old.

STAR SEEDS

Like other stars, our sun formed in a huge cloud of gas and dust. **Gravity** caused a clump of this gas and dust to gather and **compress** together. Over time, this matter formed a round, spinning mass called a protostar.

The protostar became **denser** and hotter, forming the core of the sun. After much time, the baby star stopped forming. The matter around it became the planets and other objects in our **solar system**, such as comets and asteroids.

OUT OF THIS WORLD!

The sun contains over 99 percent of all matter making up our solar system.

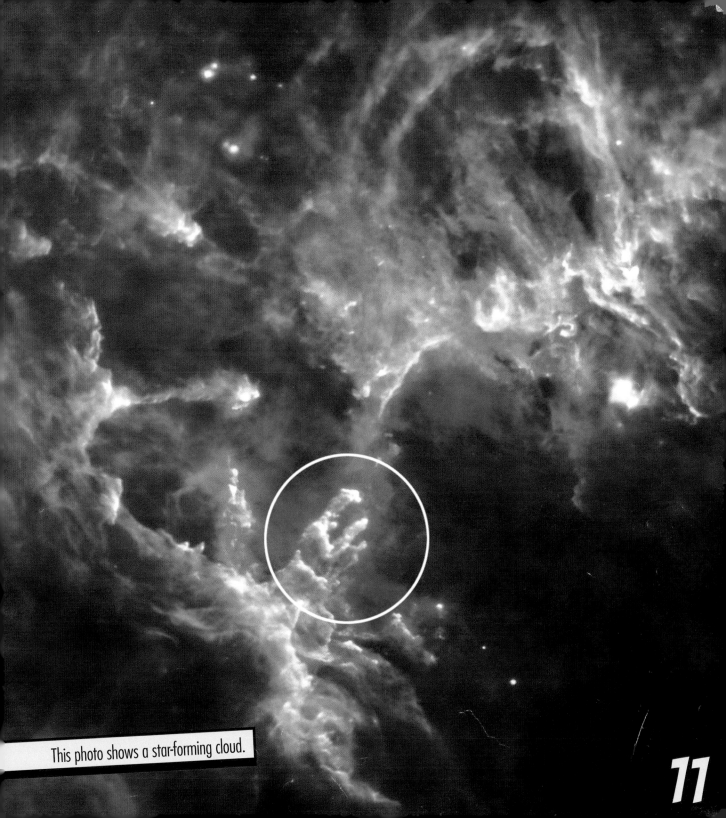

This photo shows a star-forming cloud.

WHAT'S THE MATTER?

The amount of matter a star has when it's born is an important clue to figuring out how long it will live. Stars with more mass have more **fuel** to burn—and there are some truly massive stars out there!

Scientists are continuously finding larger stars. Some measurements show the star called VY Canis Majoris may be about 2,000 times the size of our sun! If our sun were replaced by VY Canis Majoris, its surface would reach Saturn.

OUT OF THIS WORLD!

VY Canis Majoris is about 5,000 **light-years** from Earth.

VY Canis
Majoris

sun

GAS GUZZLERS

Just because VY Canis Majoris is so massive doesn't mean it will last longer than smaller stars. This is because the more massive the star is, the more fuel it burns.

You know a large truck uses more gas than a small car to drive the same distance. Similarly, a large star burns fuel more quickly than a small star. Some think VY Canis Majoris only has enough fuel left to last another few hundred thousand years.

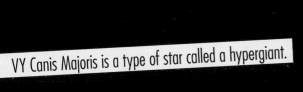

VY Canis Majoris is a type of star called a hypergiant.

15

UNDER PRESSURE

A few hundred thousand years may seem like a long time to live, but that's short when compared to our sun's lifespan. The sun has already been burning through its fuel for over 4 billion years, and it's still going strong. It produces huge amounts of energy using its most common element—hydrogen.

Because the sun is so massive, its gravitational force is strong enough to press hydrogen atoms together until they join, or fuse. This process is called nuclear fusion.

OUT OF THIS WORLD!

Some bombs use nuclear fusion to give off huge amounts of energy.

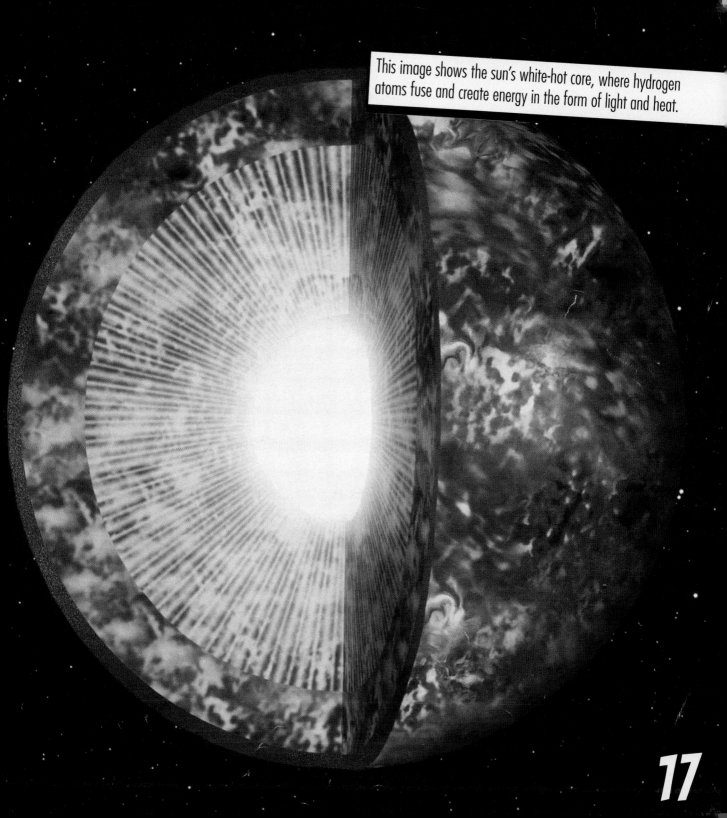

This image shows the sun's white-hot core, where hydrogen atoms fuse and create energy in the form of light and heat.

THE MAIN STAGE

The sun is in the stage of its life called the main sequence. Most of the other stars in the Milky Way are also main-sequence stars. They're in a state of balance. The stars' inward pull of gravity is matched by the outward flow of energy produced by nuclear fusion. This energy is the light and heat that we receive from the sun.

At some point, one of these forces will overpower the other. This will be the end of the sun's main-sequence stage.

OUT OF THIS WORLD!

Every second, the sun burns about 600 million tons (544 million mt) of hydrogen fuel.

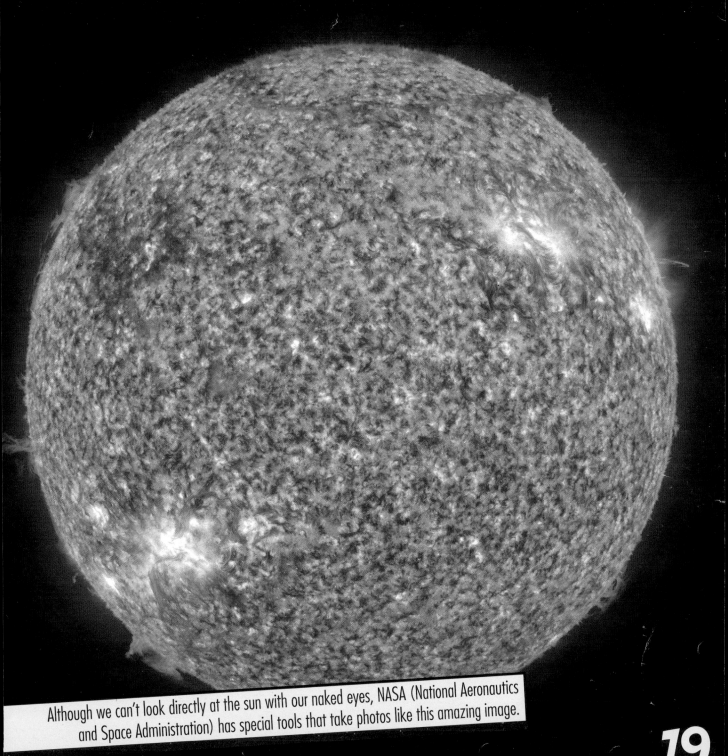

Although we can't look directly at the sun with our naked eyes, NASA (National Aeronautics and Space Administration) has special tools that take photos like this amazing image.

19

PUMP UP THE VOLUME

The sun has enough fuel to remain a main-sequence star for another 5 billion years—quite a long time! However, when the hydrogen is used up, the sun will begin to fuse helium. The sun will grow hotter and balloon outward. It will appear to be red, which is why a star at this stage is called a red giant.

As the red-giant sun grows, it will reach past the **orbits** of Mercury and Venus, the two closest planets to the sun, swallowing them.

This image shows a star in the Milky Way galaxy burning up a nearby planet (left).

HOME IS WHERE THE HEAT IS

When the sun becomes a red giant, Earth and even Mars may be swallowed up, too. Recent **research** suggests that if the enlarged sun doesn't burn up Earth, the planet may fall into the sun, where it would be destroyed by the sun's heat and gravitational pull.

It's also possible that Earth's orbit would be pushed outward, keeping the planet safe. Who knows if life will still exist on Earth then? It's hard to guess what will happen so far into the future.

Billions of years from now, Earth may be burned by the growing
sun, making it impossible for life on the surface to exist.

23

WE ARE MADE OF STARDUST

When the sun is done growing, it could be 250 times as big as it is today. Finally, it will cast off its outer layer into space. The gases of this layer will form a glowing cloud called a planetary nebula.

The matter in this cloud may one day become part of a future solar system. A planetary nebula is where the oxygen in the air we breathe and the iron in our blood came from—matter from ancient stars!

The Hubble Space Telescope has shown us what a planetary nebula looks like.

25

ONE COOL SUN

All that will remain of the sun is its hot, glowing core, which will be about the size of Earth. For the next several billion years, the sun will slowly cool down in its white-dwarf stage. As it does, it will become dimmer and gradually fade from view, like a dying campfire at night.

Far into the distant future, billions of years later, our sun will become a cold, dark ball of matter floating in space known as a black dwarf.

OUT OF THIS WORLD!

If the sun were about 10 times more massive, it could turn into a black hole after its main-sequence stage. Its gravity would be so strong that not even light could escape.

Far into the future, with no way to produce heat and light, the sun will fade from view.

OUR SUN, OUR WORLD

The sun will end its life as a black dwarf one day. The good news is this won't happen for a very, very long time. This will happen so far into the future that it won't affect our lives or the lives of anyone we know.

Our sun will live a long and productive life for billions of years to come. During its lifetime, it has made life possible in the solar system. That makes our sun a very special star indeed!

```
┌──────────────┐
│  protostar   │
└──────┬───────┘
       │
       ▼
┌──────────────┐
│ main sequence│
└──────┬───────┘
       │
       ▼
┌──────────────┐
│  red giant   │
└──────┬───────┘
       │
       ▼
┌──────────────┐
│ white dwarf  │
└──────┬───────┘
       │
       ▼
┌──────────────┐
│ black dwarf  │
└──────────────┘
```

NASA continues to use special spacecraft to study our sun so we can better understand it.

GLOSSARY

compress: to make smaller by pressing together

dense: packed very closely together

fuel: something used to make energy, heat, or power

galaxy: a large group of stars, planets, gas, and dust that form a unit within the universe

gravity: the force that pulls objects toward the center of a planet or star

light-year: the distance light travels in a year

orbit: to travel in a circle or oval around something, or the path used to make that trip

research: studying to find something new

satellite: an object that circles Earth

solar system: the sun and all the space objects that orbit it, including the planets and their moons

spiral: a shape or line that curls outward from a center point

unique: one of a kind

FOR MORE INFORMATION

BOOKS

Abramson, Andra Serlin, and Mordecai-Mark Mac Low. *Inside Stars*. New York, NY: Sterling Children's Books, 2011.

Chrismer, Melanie. *The Sun*. New York, NY: Children's Press, 2005.

Morris, Rick. *Stars and Planets*. Lincolnwood, IL: Publications International, 2010.

WEBSITES

Sun and Earth Background
stargazers.gsfc.nasa.gov/resources/sun_earth_background.htm
Find out how the features of the sun affect Earth.

Why Do We Study the Sun?
www.nasa.gov/vision/universe/solarsystem/sun_for_kids_main.html
Read more about why we study the sun.

INDEX